(End Papers)
Wall fresco, Dunhuang – Gansu

(Previous page)
1. Between Lhasa and Gyangze – Tibet

2. Potala Palace, Lhasa – Tibet

(Following pages)
3. Gansu Desert, Dunhuang – Gansu

HAN SUYIN'S
CHINA

PHOTOGRAPHS BY MIKE LANGFORD & GEOFF MASON

UNIVERSE BOOKS
New York

Published in the United States of America in 1988 by
Universe Books 381 Park Avenue South, New York,
N.Y. 10016

© Text: Han Suyin 1987
© Photographs: Mike Langford/Geoff Mason 1987

Designed and produced for the Publisher by
J.M. McGregor Pty Ltd
PO Box 6990 Gold Coast Mail Centre,
Queensland 4217, Australia

Library of Congress Cataloging-in-Publication Data

Han, Suyin, pseud.
    Han Suyin's China.

1. Han, Suyin, pseud.—Journeys—China. 2. China—
Description and travel—1976–   . 3. Authors, English—
20th century—Journeys—China. I. Langford, Michael
1933–   . II. Mason, Geoff. III. title. PR6015.A4674Z463
1987   915.1'0458   88–1171
ISBN 0-87663-688-1

Typeset by: Keyset Phototype, Sydney
Printed by: South China Printing Company, Hong Kong

CHINA: her size roughly that of Canada or the United States. Her population one billion one hundred million, 22 per cent of the planet's human beings.

China: very young, 60 per cent of the Chinese under 25 years of age. Very old, millennia of accumulated and still potent history, pride of remembered greatness motivating her march towards the new technological era which is changing the world, and changing her.

China: her history not unitary, but made up of many histories; as she is made up of many different peoples, altogether 56 nations. Yet she is a Oneness, coherent, whole. THE GREAT WITHIN.

There is a China of the plains, easily travelled, a tourist delight. Here are the wealthiest, the most advanced metropolises: Beijing, Tienjin, Shanghai, Nanjing, Guangzhou . . . fertile alluvial lowlands which seem vast, yet are less than 15 per cent of her total territory. And China's arable, cultivable acres make up only seven per cent of the world's total acreage. On this she feeds almost a quarter of the world's people. A prodigious achievement!

This China of the plains stretches from Manchuria to Hong Kong; most of it lies eastwards, with easy access to the ocean. Here both urban and rural areas have greatly profited from the recent economic reforms. Most of the foreign investments, the special economic zones, the new industrial plants, are sited here. Here are the skills, the manpower, the markets, the communication network. Most of the universities are also here, and more than 80 per cent of the population. Prosperity is evident — over 60 per cent of new houses in the villages, over 20 per cent of families with television installed in the last ten years, large new apartment houses for urban dwellers, modern hotels . . .

But there is the other China, 85 per cent of the total surface of the land. This China is not easily visited, for communication is still a problem. It stretches in an immense bow from North to South, and in it live, besides the 'typical' Chinese, who call themselves the Hans, fifty-odd other races or ethnic groups, called 'national minorities'. These hark back to China's very beginning. With them the Hans both warred and traded; co-existed, intermarried or ostracized, for nearly 5,000 years.

This other China has many mountain ranges, thousand kilometre long chains stretching from west to east dividing the land into enclosed plateaus and basins whose *rivers never reach any sea. It has many deserts; more than a million square kilometres of deserts — almost 15 per cent of her total area of nine million six hundred thousand square kilometres. It has immense grasslands and steppes, oases and salt lakes, jungles and troughs lower than the Dead Sea in Palestine.*

This China we must know in order really to know China. It is this conglomerate of many nations, mosaic of peoples, languages and customs, which shaped Chinese culture as we know it today and it is in developing and modernising this area that her future lies.

North, Northwest, Southwest . . . for administrative purposes, this other China, nearly seven million out of the nearly ten million square kilometres of the land, is conveniently divided into regions, each one holding several provinces. I have walked, ridden, jeeped, explored this China several times in the course of the last three decades. I have learnt the local names of mountains, rivers, deserts; for everything here has two names, the Han Chinese name, and the name (or names) given by the national minorities which inhabit the area.

Mountains: the majestic Altai, whence came thudding on thick-legged Mongol ponies so many nomad hordes. The Bogden or Heaven's mountains, sitting in vast skirts of their own crumbled stone. From their slopes flow streams feeding the oases strung along the rim of inland deserts. The Kunlun and the Karakoram, the Pamir and the Himalayas — here Mount Everest is known as Chomolungma.

Deserts: the stone deserts of the Gobi and the Ordos, the Tanguli and the Kurban Tungu and the dreadful Taklamakan.

Plateaus and basins: Dzungaria and Tarim and Tsaidam, and the Roof of the World, the immense plateau of Tibet.

THE NORTH AND NORTHWEST

GANSU, the Long Corridor, is one of China's most fascinating provinces. It is the route from the plains of the GREAT WITHIN to Central Asia, and is shaped like a long dumb-bell (hence the name of corridor), one knob spreading in the Asian land mass, the southern knob connecting with Mongolia, the Southwest, and lowland China. It will become the centre of an immense web of communication spanning the Asian mainland. With its area of 455,000 square kilometres, it has a population under 24 million, of whom three quarters are Han and one quarter are minorities.

The Long Corridor is where the Han race began. So claim the legends, the myths, and which archaeological research confirms from thousands of early sites found here, dating back 7 to 9,000 years.

Through the Long Corridor runs the Yellow River, the Huang He , cradle of the Han race. The soil is called Huang Tu , Yellow earth; it is loess, soil ground fine as talcum by the churning of Arctic winds blowing from the Siberian steppes.

Loess is fertile, but has no structural stability; rain and wind carve it into cliffs and gullies. The slightest shock can bring vertical cleavage and an avalanche burying valleys and fields. There is 580,000 square kilometres of this loess, extending across North China, and growing aridity threatens to turn it into desert.

The Huang He winds its silt-laden waters through the loess. It is the most destructive and muddiest stream in the world. Over 5,000 kilometres long, it has breached its dykes 1,700 times in a recorded two and a half millennia, and changed course eight times. Disastrous stream, drowning millions, China's sorrow, its bed forever rises due to the loess silt and is now 32 metres above the cities in its lower reaches.

Yet the Han love their monster river and it is probably due to the age-long struggle with it that they became skilled tillers, hardy, enduring, totally bent on survival. Their earliest heroes were men who tamed the waters, deflected floods, dug canals, and saved the people. Chinese culture is 'hydraulic' says the famous scholar Wittfogel. This means that water being paramount for survival, the social structure must be cohesive, able to mobilise labour power to build dams and levees, dig drainage canals and reservoirs, remove mountains and reshape the earth. This means an authoritarian government, where the sovereign is judged by his ability to provide food, where natural disasters are imputed to his own personal defects. Indeed, such is China's basic philosophy of government, until today.

It was the loess culture that invented the ideogram. Inscriptions carved 5,000 years ago on oracle bones (scapulae of ox, carapace of tortoise) and which can still be read today, enquire "Will the rains come?" "Will the banks of the river hold fast?" It was here that so many of the skills were evolved: the art of bronze, spinning and silk (2,700 b.c.), ceramic, porcelain, metal alloys, the building of cities four square in harmony with the cardinal points.

The Hans prospered, multiplied, pushed eastwards, southwards, plainwards, pushing off the rich alluvial lands the softer-bred ethnic groups they encountered, who retreated to uplands and valleys where we find them today. The Han did not expand northwest, not only because of the lack of cultivable soil, but also because of the presence of hunters and herders, nomads driving great flocks requiring forever fresh pastures, later moving on horseback in the land ocean of Central Asia, and soon becoming pillagers of the settled plains.

Chinese annals record these invaders. First of all the Huns, Xuing Nu in Chinese, four millennia ago or more, who left mountains of skulls behind them and boasted that no grass grew under their horses' hooves. Europe would also know, under Attila, the Scourge of God, the Hun armies who in later centuries almost reached Paris.

The Huns disappeared, but after them came many others; Tanguts and Turkomans and Khitans and Tatars and Toba and Kirghiz . . . hordes with feet of oxen and others with black carriages (the latter possibly the Scythians whom Alexander of Macedon also encountered, with black tents upon their oxcarts?). Many centuries later came the Mongols under Gengis Khan, conquering Russia and India and also China. Gengis Khan's grave is here, in the Ordos desert, where he crossed to invade the GREAT WITHIN. A Mongol dynasty (Yuan dynasty 1271-1368 a.d.) ruled from today's Beijing. Still later came the Manchus, who ruled China as the Tsing dynasty from 1644 to 1911, when China became a Republic.

Conquerors, invaders; founding dynasties, morselling the GREAT WITHIN, but inevitably and swiftly — so swiftly, sometimes within ten years, or twenty becoming synthesized, educated by their subjects, shaped by that fascinating, overwhelming culture. Many have simply disappeared, or merged, or become 'national minorities'. It is here, in the Long Corridor, that so many of these epic wars were waged, alliances made and broken. From Gansu the armies of the GREAT WITHIN marched out to do battle with the Barbarians. Thus the Han dynasty (206 b.c. to 220 a.d.) from which the Chinese take their name, conquered the oases of Central Asia and garrisoned them, sent embassies to the many kingdoms lying between the Corridor and the Caspian, and recorded these occurrences in maps and memoirs — there are living, historical monuments of this outward thrust: the Great Wall and the Silk Road. Where it furrows the desertic plains here the wall dates back to 305 b.c.

Work on the Great Wall went on for many centuries, and cost millions of lives. It stops at Yumen, the Gate of Jade, where the deserts begin, the "place of shifting sands" described on old maps with sand dunes 40 metres high "where no spring blossoms, and only the corpses of men and animals are seen". The Wall was protection against invasion, against sand, but also for the camel caravans travelling the Imperial Highways built by the Hans, bringing silk to Tyre and Sidon, and to Rome.

The stalwart tourist gifted with stamina, time and curiosity, should do the Wall here in Gansu. From Tianshui, Heaven's Water, where the fabulous Maidzi Mountain is carved in and out with Buddhist figures, to Lanzhou, Orchid city, a trading centre established 81 b.c. and today capital of the province. Lanzhou is beautiful, set on a plateau: below it winds the Yellow River, really ochre-brown.

It has fine parks, avenues, a marvellous museum (palaeo and neolithic discoveries), and a modern university with a department of nuclear physics where several Nobel Prize winners have come to teach.

On to Wine Fountain, a quaint and lovely town renowned for the jade mined here, called 'light in the darkness', carved in cups and goblets which, it is said, turn colour should the drink be poisonous.

5.   Lhasa – Tibet

6. Lhasa – Tibet

7. Citadel at Gyangze – Tibet

8. Polkor Monastery, Gyangze – Tibet

(Following page)
9. Potala Palace, Lhasa – Tibet

10.   Tea house, Sera Monastery, Lhasa – Tibet

11.　Meat roasting, Lhasa – Tibet

12.   Lhasa – Tibet

13.   Kashgar – Xinjiang

14.   Prayer Seller, Lhasa – Tibet

15. Between Lhasa and Gyangze – Tibet

Westwards to the fabulous Buddhist caves of Dunhuang, 460 extraordinary caves dating back to the third century a.d., covered with frescoes and paintings and once full of statues (alas, many stolen, others destroyed). No one should miss Dunhuang, though now tourists only stay a day or two, when a month is not enough. And here is history painted for all to see: merchants and princes, adventurers and camel boys, monks and preachers from a hundred kingdoms and a thousand nations, upon the walls. Hooknosed Syrians carrying wine gourds of goatskin; bearded merchants with pearls and cinnabar and large birds' eggs (ostrich eggs); embassies with Arab horses and lions and unicorns; African pygmies and jugglers from Alexandria; fire-eaters from Benares and bishops from Byzantium . . . anything new delighted the Hans, who took to felt hats and peacock feathers, crowded to watch elephants and cheetahs, learnt strange music and foreign dances, and quaint fashions in dress . . . as they do today. This happened because the Turkoman nomads who followed the stupid Huns were intelligent and adaptable, settling in oases, making alliances with the Chinese dynasties. There is even a whisper, from unorthodox historians, that the first emperor of the Tang dynasty (618 to 907 a.d.) was half a Turkoman.

Along the Imperial Highway came religion and refugees. Nestorians and Manicheans; Zoroastrians and Jews. The latter still have a settlement in the Chinese city of Kaifeng.

There is also the lost Roman legion, with whose descendants I was to eat figs and flat bread at a village near Dunhuang. Buddhist monks travelled back and forth between India and China for many centuries. In the sixth century came the Arab Muslims; admitted and allowed to settle in China because their religion was 'truthful and pure'.

Thus, the Northwest, through the Long Corridor of Gansu, became a centre for culture and communication. A reservoir also, of today's national minorities. More than a quarter of Gansu's population is Hui, the name given to Muslims, descendants of Arab or Persian settlers. In Lanzhou there is a Muslim township with 56 mosques, including one exclusively for women.

The Long Corridor is an exciting place, and now with factories, a petrochemical plant (there is oil at the Jade Gate) and aluminium works, it is an industrial centre. But it is threatened with desertification, as is all of North China. Here are institutes for reafforestation and for checking the desert. The loess hills are being terraced and planted with scrub, bushes and grasses, which can be used as fuel to spare the remaining forests. Like every province in China, Gansu wants to modernise; it sends delegations abroad; it is building hydro- electric dams, for it needs energy. Roads and railways have been built in the last twenty years. From here we can start to explore that other China, until now so remote.

XINJIANG, The New Domain

MIRAGES *and mosques, and Bactrian camels, who can sniff underground water, and an approaching sandstorm. The sun blazes down upon our jeep as we drive to Hami, following the Silk Road Imperial Highway (northern branch). I see sails and palm trees: mirage, for there is no water. Hami's rainfall is a scarce one centimetre a year. We are in the desert and in the outskirts of the city a herd of wild donkeys gallops past. Donkey carts were used by the silver merchants of East China coming to trade, but now jeeps and trucks and lorries replace them.*

Hami is an old stopping place of the Northern Imperial Highway, and now an industrial city. A canal brings water from the mountains north of it. Hami is 200 metres below sea level, lower than the Dead Sea. It is most famous all over China for its melons, sold even in Hong Kong.

From Hami through the desert, the air tasting like a furnace, to Turfan. Turfan is 160 metres below sea level and not far away are the Mountains of Fire, with the dried up salt lakes terrible to cross "full of evil demons and hot winds, not a bird in the air above, nor an animal on the ground below". But Turfan is an oasis, famous in the past as Kocho, or Karakocho, with Nestorian, Manichean and Buddhist relics strewn about, and today many mosques.

Here the population is 100 per cent Turkoman, or Uighurs, as the five million Turkomans living in this province are called. "The Romans, the Arabs and the Uighur Turks .. were all known as great grape growers and drinkers of wine" writes an English historian. And Turfan still today is famous for its grapes. Here the link between the Persian empire of yore, and the GREAT WITHIN *is very evident; as it will be throughout Xinjiang.*

The low clay houses, the mosques, the courtyards . . . one could be in any town of the Muslim world. But here is music, and singing, even when the air is incandescent with heat. The girls are not veiled, they move beautiful and free in striped dresses. The men are handsome with jaunty embroidered caps upon their heads.

In the evening we go to the grape orchards and sit below the golden hanging fruit. We eat roast mutton on skewers and flat bread called samoza , and dance to the music of tambourines and flutes. All the Uighurs are remarkable dancers and this too is a tradition. Turfan not only used to send the famous 'mare teat', oval grapes, translucent and golden, to the Chinese court, packed in snow containers kept cool with ice outside (in the fifth century a.d.!!), but also "the best musicians and dancers in the world" or so say the Chinese records.

An underground system of wells and canals (to prevent evaporation in the fierce heat) comes from Persia, and so do the songs, and the music. These influenced Han music and poetry. In fact some Chinese lyrical poetry is still called 'Persian'.

From Turfan to Urumqi , the capital of Xinjiang. And here we get the full story of the New Domain. Back and forth, during the centuries, came and went Han rule, but only in the 1750's was this area finally incorporated in the Chinese empire. After that, attempts to 'detach' the New Domain were made by the Russians for some decades; for Xinjiang, though difficult of access from the GREAT WITHIN, is very near to today's Asian republics of the USSR. In fact, on both sides of the border, the people are the same. For here are the Uighurs, Kazakhs, Kirghiz and Tadjiks and other Turkoman tribes; and over the border are Uzbekhistan, Kazakstan, Tajikiztan and Kirghizstan . . . and there are memories of a common history.

Urumqi is in the northern basin of Xinjiang, called Dzungaria, divided by the Bogdan or Heavenly mountains from the southern basin, or Tarim. Here the Hans have put to use uninhabited and uncultivated land, again by using the streams from the mountains which otherwise lost themselves into the desert sands. Both basins have a central desert area. There is much potential here in Szungaria, and Urumqi has textiles and factories (tractors) and coal mines, and oil from the Karamai oil fields. There is also good grassland in the northern valleys for cattle grazing.

Xinjiang, 1,646,800 square kilometres, one sixth of China, contains scarcely ten million people, of whom five million are Uighurs and three million Han; the rest being Kirghiz, Kazaks, Tadjiks, Uzbeks, Hui, Mongols (from previous Mongol dynasty garrisons) . . . altogether twelve minorities, of whom seven are Muslim. Prospecting reveals good stores of coal, iron, gold, other minerals. The cotton fields are supplying cotton for textile factories; the grasslands need development . . . there must be more manpower, but importing the only available manpower, which is Han labour (and chiefly from Sichuan province, as we shall see), may produce friction.

Meanwhile American mining companies are here, to consider extraction of minerals. The railway from Beijing through Lanzhou and Hami stops at Urumqi , but now may be prolonged to join the trans-Siberian network. There are universities, teachers' colleges and schools. The Uighur language is closely akin to Turkish and romanization has been introduced. "We must have Uighur scientists, doctors, astronomers" say the Uighurs, who know their own history well and for whom the term: 'national minority' is irksome. "We were great kingdoms" one of them told me. Like other minorities, the Uighurs are allowed up to three children (often they have more) whereas the Han enforce family planning for themselves, restricting to one child per couple.

Here, as elsewhere among the autonomous regions, an effort is being made to train local cadres to run local affairs. It is fairly successful in Xinjiang, which is well represented at the Congresses in Beijing.

We go up the Bogdan mountains to see the Kazakhs who have great flocks of horses and cattle and live in tents on the mountains. Here is abundant water from mountain lakes, and the Kazakhs live in tents lined with rugs. We sit with them and drink fermenting mare's milk, which the women churn in big copper pots, and eat hard cheese. There must be scientific herding, the Kazakhs say. But many of the young ones do not wish to herd, they prefer to go to Urumqi and find a job in the new factories.

Xinjiang's southern basin is composed almost entirely of the one million square kilometre Taklamakan desert, a word which means "You get in but you cannot get out". The Taklamakan is rimmed by oases. One river, the Tarim, has been channelled by the Han Chinese to irrigate farms; saxaul and tamarisk and sand figs protect the fields, and there are lines of poplars along the canals. Some sixty thousand youths from Shanghai were sent here to develop the land. However, the coastal people dread the desert, and many have now returned to their own city.

A new effort is being made to inspire young people to come to the New Domain, here to work and to settle. They will earn twice the salaries they would get on the coast, and their children will be promised entrance to the best universities of Eastern China . . .

On to Kashgar, a name of fabulous memory; renowned, along with Bokhara and Samarkand, in so many Thousand and One Night tales. Marco Polo came here. "It contains many towns and castles . . . the people are Mohammedan . . . they subsist by commerce and manufacture . . . merchants from this country travel to all parts of the world." He noted Nestorian Christians, who had their own churches.

Kashgar today is two cities as indeed applies throughout Xinjiang old and new. In the one the women dress as in Marco Polo's day, swathed in mantles and covered heads; in the other young Kashgarians wear leather jackets and jeans, and want to drive the lorries and trucks which, today, stop here on the road to Pakistan. There are bazaars which appear not to have changed for a thousand years, with pottery and brass jugs and embroidered saddle bags and leather slippers, and next to them shops with nylon shirts and transistor radios and television sets and model refrigerators from Shanghai.

The mosques are splendid. There are mosques for Uighurs and mosques for the Hui (Chinese Moslems) who do not understand Arabic. I visit the tomb of the Perfumed Lady, the beautiful woman loved by Tsien Lung the Emperor, (1735-1795), who was sent all the way from Kashgar to Beijing to become his favourite. For her he made his Jesuit architects build a western style palace and a mosque in the Imperial Palaces, which alas were burnt down by the troops of England and France in 1860.

There is a resurrection of Kashgar's famous rugs, which since the 15th century have been much prized for their mixture of Chinese and Persian designs, and are known in the trade as 'samarkands'. But above all Kashgar will once again become a centre for communication, as the Silk Road is once again active. Its southern sector goes across the mountain passes to Pakistan, to today's Islamabad.

17. Lake Tianchi – Xinjiang

18. Kashgar – Xinjiang

19. Kashgar – Xinjiang

20.   Hami melons in Turfan – Xinjiang

21.   Pool players, Kashgar – Xinjiang

22. ' Ping Pong ', Urumqi – Xinjiang

23. Kazakh herdsmen, Tianchi – Xinjiang

26. Silk sellers, Urumqi – Xinjiang

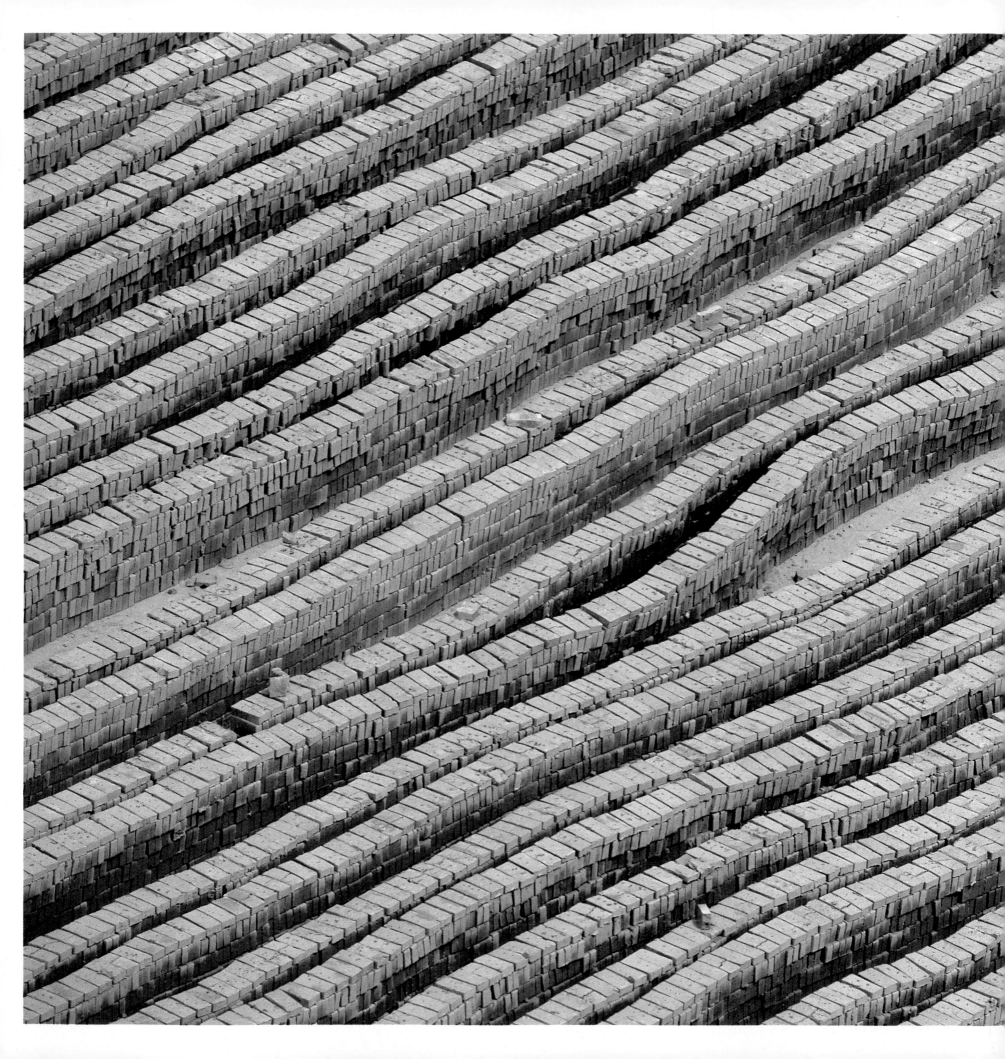

27.   Bricks drying, Turfan – Xinjiang

28.   Morning, Kashgar – Xinjiang

29.   Sunday market, Kashgar – Xinjiang

30.   Shopkeepers, Urumqi – Xinjiang

31. Gansu Desert, Dunhuang – Gansu

32. Gansu Desert, Dunhuang – Gansu

33.   Uighur children, Kashgar – Xinjiang

34.　Uighur dancers, Turfan – Xinjiang.

Tourists can travel it although it takes stamina to cross the high passes, where the wind is fierce and the peaks are brushed black with not a speck of snow left upon them. Lorries come and go; maintenance men and surveyors, mostly Han, cheer the caravans on wheels. Solitary eagles circle watchfully as we leave Xinjiang, the New Domain. From Kashgar, going southwards, one not only reaches the Indian subcontinent, but one can also cross over, at more than 4,000 metres, into Tibet — the Roof of the World.

TIBET, *The Roof of the World*

AT an average of 4,000 metres the Tibetan plateau is crossed by yet higher ranges. Tibet, 1,220,000 square kilometres, is vastly uninhabited; only some southern valleys, such as the Lhasa one, are settled. There are clusters of herdsmen tending yaks at round 4,000 metres, but above that height women do not conceive easily. The herdsmen here practise polyandry, to keep the flocks together, one woman marrying all the brothers of one family . . . this also does not improve the birthrate. Tibet has a population under 2 million, of whom 1.5 million are Tibetans (including Khambas of the south). More Tibetans (2 million) live outside Tibet proper, in Qinghai, also in Sichuan province in the southwest.

The origin of the Tibetans has been debated. Old maps show the province north of Tibet, today known as Qinghai, the Azure Sea, also called Upper Tibet, as inhabited by the Jiang, yet another minority today, (no more than 300,000). I have visited them, lovably energetic, greatly gifted as wood carvers. The Tibetans are mixed with Jiang and also Tangut nomads, as well as southern races from the Himalayan region.

There are, however, vastly different lifestyles between today's Tibetans and the Jiang and other minorities. The Jiang grow maize and excellent apples; their houses are flat roofed, they have lovely carved windows and doors. The difference lies in religion, which has totally conditioned Tibetans for a thousand years.

In 640 a.d. King Songtsang Kampo of Tibet united the various tribes and married a Chinese princess, who brought porcelain, ceramic, silk, music, architects, and the Buddhist religion to Lhasa. The famous Jokhang temple of Lhasa was built and other temples followed.

By the tenth century there were some ten million Tibetans. They spilled over into other provinces, even attempted to capture the GREAT WITHIN's capital city. But after the 14th century their numbers declined rapidly, and this decline is greatly due to their religious practices.

Religion is the core, the very reason for life in Tibet. Buddhist practice here integrated pre-Buddhist elements of shamanism, sorcery. "Unseen demons inhabit every tree, rock, stream . . . not a gesture, not a word, but could draw malevolence . . .

which only the prayers of the priests can exorcise . . ." but these prayers are paid for. A religious caste of lamas (monks) arose, superseding all lay authority. Under a shrewd and ruthless pontiff, the founder of the Yellow Sect, Tibet remained, until the communist revolution in 1949, authoritarian theocracy. Fully one quarter of the males were recruited for the monasteries. Serfdom was the lot of the peasants, who cultivated the lands owned by the immensely wealthy monasteries. Tibet was kept closed to any outside influence, although there was to be a Chinese 'governor' posted there since the 13th century. No wheel except the wheel of the prayer mills; everything was brought in on the backs of men, loads of salt, brick tea, sugar, from the Chinese provinces, climbing up, up, up to the 4 kilometre high plateau.

It was in 1260 that, under the Mongols, Tibet was officially attached to China. The Mongols became converted to the Tibetan brand of Buddhism, and they and the Manchus entertained close links with the hierarchy. Tibetan temples were built in Beijing. To strengthen his grip on Tibet, emperor Tsien Lung (1735 to 1798) devised the policy of the Golden Urn. Whenever a Dalai Lama, supreme religious pontiff, died, a search for the infant boy in which he had reincarnated took place. This led to much intrigue and even murders, and so the Chinese emperor set up a Gold Urn at the Jokhang. The names of potential reincarnees, chosen by the dreams of diviners, were written upon tallies and placed in it.

The choice was made by the Panchen Lama (representing the temporal affairs pontiff of Tibet) dipping a hand in the presence of the Chinese governor. If the successor for a Panchen Lama was sought, it was the Dalai Lama who put a hand in the urn.

In 1950 the Chinese communist armies entered Tibet and though guaranteeing that the Tibetans could go on practising their religion, it was soon obvious that the system could not continue. The Chinese built roads right across Tibet, linking Lhasa both to the Azure Sea and to Sichuan, also to Kashgar in Xinjiang. They built the first maternity hospital in 1954 — previously serf women had their babies in cow byres. The infant mortality was of course extremely high, and that, and polyandry, and so many boys becoming monks, were probably the reasons for the Tibetans, like the Mongols, decreasing in number. Other attempted reforms began to erode the power of the monasteries — knocking the chains off the feet of the serfs for instance. A rebellion took place. The Dalai Lama left with his retinue, but the Panchen Lama remained.

Today, after 20 years of repression, the Tibetan religion is once again countenanced. Monasteries which were destroyed are being rebuilt. But this is another era. The monks no longer own land, nor is their power as great as it was. However, religion is still very strong in the heart of the Tibetans. One only has to go to Lhasa to see it.

Lhasa, full of temples, dominated by the formidable Potala (one thousand rooms, once the residence of the Dalai Lama), is full of pilgrims, Tibetans from all over China. For to come to Lhasa is to ensure bliss, nirvana, an end to suffering and to rebirth.

I have seen them, on today's roads, pilgrims walking — though some now come in buses and lorries. It is the act of walking which is blessed, and very pious Tibetans even prostrate themselves every step of the way — it takes them three to five years to reach Lhasa. "We have to look after them . . . set up inns, have doctors on hand. Some of the women give birth on the road" — thus an harassed official told me on the occasion of a recent pilgrimage, when 200,000 Tibetans were on the move.

Will Tibet change? Yes, but not very quickly. The Han Chinese are cautious. They know that they cannot hurry the 'brother minorities', for this only provokes anger and revolt. The government is still subsidising Tibet, for agriculture is lagging here. It is still difficult to enforce rules of hygiene. The disposal of corpses is done by 'Heavenly burial', i.e. the cadaver is exposed on mountain slopes, to be eaten by carrion birds. No Tibetan will ever eat fish, though the rivers are full of fish. Today's young Tibetans are loath to become monks. They prefer to become tourist guides, or tradesmen, now that the road to Nepal is open and an active commerce in coral and turquoise necklaces and tankas, or holy pictures, goes on. Tibetan writers have started writing novels instead of writing prayer tracts and last year 'Romeo and Juliet', translated into Tibetan, was performed on television for Tibetan viewers.

One cannot help liking the Tibetans. They are so vital, so cheerful . . . perhaps because nothing matters, save to assure one's salvation through prayer, pilgrimage and the burning of much butter in lamps before the Gods. And one cannot help falling in love with the yaks, that splendid animal which provides everything needed, meat and milk and butter and clothing and leather — and which below 2,000 metres of altitude becomes quite sick.

QUINGHAI, The Azure Sea

QUINGHAI is an unexplored paradise. Its name derives from Lake Kokonor, a Tangut word. Qinghai lake is startlingly sapphire blue. It is the largest salt lake in China, 4,500 sq kms, and it is the stopping place for millions of migratory birds, swans, cormorants, wild geese and brown headed gulls. The Azure Sea also has the famous Kumbum Tibetan temple, where the supreme pontiff of the Yellow Sect was born in the 13th century. Here are the carved and painted butter figures (two tons of butter used) which are redone every year, when hundreds of thousands of pilgrims congregate to celebrate their religion's founder.

Immense grasslands are here, untouched, capable of sustaining a great deal of cattle . . . and therefore giving China much protein. But the Azure Sea, area 721,000 sq kilometres, has only four million people, 60 per cent of them being Han, settled round the cultivated lower land. Besides Tibetans there are Hui, Jiang, Mongol, Du and Salar (a Turkoman tribe akin to the Uighurs) and there are altogether 185 Tibetan temples and 811 mosques in the province. The new governor of the province is a geologist, 42 years old.

Both in Tibet and Qinghai teams of scientists, geologists, and prospectors are exploring. The Azure Sea apparently holds rare metals in large quantities, and there are plans for development. So too, in Tibet, there are plans to tap the tremendous thermal energy (hot springs) and also hydro-electric power. For from this Roof of the World issue all the great rivers of China, Thailand, Burma, Bangladesh, North India and Pakistan. The Huang He, Yangtse, Mekong, the Menam, the Salween and Irawaddy, the Brahmaputra and the Indus . . . 90 per cent or more of China's potential electric power lies in this region and of course the Roof of the World is a great strategic area. From here satellites can be launched far more easily than lower down. The study of the Universe, with giant telescopes, could also be helped by the altitude.

THE SOUTHWEST
SICHUAN, Province of the Four Streams

DOWN from Tibet, either by road (a week) or by air (3 hours), to Chengdu, capital of Sichuan province, the most populous province in China. Here the soil seems alive, breathing with toil and sweat and manure. Here are the most hardworking people of China.

Sichuan, the Four Streams, is also known as the Garden of Abundance, China's granary, landlocked paradise. It was early open to Han culture, despite the difficulty of communication. Settlements occurred from the Gansu Long Corridor and since then Sichuan has been, culturally as well as economically, the very heart of China, fortress and refuge for many of its poets and scholars in times of invasion and distress, feeding, when needed, provinces that were famished. Even as recently as twenty years ago Sichuan was still feeding five other provinces which were 'deficitary' in grain.

Sichuan's population is 100 million people, ten per cent of China, for an area of 560,000 sq kilometres, equivalent to that of France. Most of the population is Han, and most of the Hans are in the Red Basin, which is the most densely populated area in all China. Once a seabed, it is ensconced in a ring of mountains, hence its landlocked repute. "Oh the roads of this land are hard . . . harder than to climb to Heaven" wrote one of China's most famous poets. Which had not stopped him from coming here where he found solace, refuge, learning and many friends.

38. Herbalist, Chongqing – Sichuan

39.   Upper reaches of Yellow River – Gansu

40. Train travel, Kunming to Chengdu in Sichuan

41. Xining to Golmud railway – Qinghai

42.   Terracotta Warrior Ballet, Xian – Shaanxi

43.   Peking Opera – Beijing

44.   Terracotta Warrior Ballet, Xian – Shaanxi

Through one of our planet's quirks, the mountain ranges which were proceeding west to east suddenly here bunch up and run north to south at right angles to their previous course, carrying with them the main rivers of southeast Asia. Only one, the Yangtse river, pursues a difficult, rock-hewing, cliff-banked course eastwards. It is the main — and a difficult — way of egress from the province. Difficult because of the famous Yangtse gorges, a tourist's delight, but an impediment to navigation.

Just before the gorges is the city of Chongqing. Chongqing will become, one day, of paramount importance as China's greatest inland port, but at the moment it is struggling. Struggling since the last 35 years to dynamite the rocks in the middle of the Yangtse river gorges, to widen the narrow, ductlike passages of the monster river, which canyons its way to the plains 2,000 odd kilometres away.

The fertility of the Red Basin was man-made. Just as the Huang He was tamed beginning round the 21st century b.c., the catastrophic torrents tumbling from the Roof of the World, tributaries of the Yangtse river were here canalized, stopping the stone and silt hurtling down. A total reshaping of the land, a prodigious engineering feat, unique in the world, was performed.

It was in 320 b.c. that the work of dredging the streams coming down into the Red Basin began. It was 250 b.c. when a genius engineer, Li Ping, cut a mountain in two, dividing the river, then built a breach-proof rockwalled course for the streams, and dykes and dams, to regulate the flow. Altogether, 2,000 dykes, 10 trunk canals, 520 branch canals, a network totalling 1,200 kilometres, which can be seen today if the tourist drives 40 odd kilometres from Chengdu, the capital city. From this complex more canals and canalicules derived a vascular system similar to the body's, networking the Red Basin, keeping it fertile for 20 centuries.

Today, the method then used of making dykes out of baskets of woven bamboo filled with the egg-shaped stones which the rivers bring down, is still in use. The network is kept up, for upon it depends the livelihood, not of 100 million, but of many more, for Sichuan continues to be the granary of China.

There are temples to Li Ping, the engineer, and to his son, who continued his work; delightful in their tenth century architecture. I can think of no other spot where China's culture, seeking Harmony between Nature and Man, is more obvious.

From the 5th century and onwards the whole of the Yangtse river basin became the key economic area of the GREAT WITHIN.

The increasingly arid North, however, with Beijing as capital, remained the political centre. There is a saying in China, "When the capital moves south, the Emperor becomes soft, and the GREAT WITHIN is lost".

What can one say of Sichuan, which does not sound excessive? For here, in this province, China's greatest poets either were born or came to live; the best scholars, and even in recent, contemporary China the most eminent painters.

The Chengdu academy of painting, the academy of music, are well able to keep up with Shanghai. Here is a tradition of culture, of civilisation, deeply ingrained in the people. "In Sichuan every man is a poet, but also a warrior."

In every town flourish tea houses, meeting places for talk, speculation; for story tellers who tell great tales of the past. Everywhere there is Sichuan opera, far more lively than the much admired, but rigidly classical, Beijing opera. Not only are there choruses as in Greek tragedies, but the singers ad lib freely, often mixing satirical comments on the contemporary scene with old classical themes . . . to bring down the house with laughter. Here is garrulity and humour, and also an enormous sense of being truly China's 'winning card'. Sichuan resisted the Mongols and the Manchus for decades, far longer than any other province. In Chongqing one can still see the battlements of an old fort, which stood against Gengis Khan's armies for many years.

During the Second World War, when the Japanese overran and occupied the whole of China of the plains, it was Sichuan which harboured the Chinese government and fed 40 million refugees, who streamed in from the invaded provinces. The refugees included the main universities from Beijing, Tienjin, Shanghai . . . students and their professors, who walked thousands of kilometres away from the invader, reaching Sichuan. Here teaching went on for the eight years during which the war lasted (China's war began in 1937).

It was in Chongqing, at the head of the Yangtse gorges, that the Government of Free China established itself. Chongqing was repeatedly bombed, 90 per cent of the city destroyed . . . and rebuilt. (I was there.) Today the air raid tunnels burrowing the hillsides are used as markets, shops, discos and strobe-lit nightspots.

It is from Sichuan that some of the famous generals of the Long March came, including today's great man of China, Deng Xiaoping.

Sichuan poetry, Sichuan painters, Sichuan cuisine and wines — restaurants presenting this hot, spicy cooking flourish all over the world. The export of Sichuan chefs is a thriving business for the province. Sichuan's universities, especially her medical school and school of dentistry, are among the best in China.

Here the past and the present come together, one reinforcing the other. Hence Sichuan, though so far from the coast, though with so many transport difficulties, is by no means 'backward'.

Perhaps this is due to a strange historical phenomenon. Sichuan was actually depopulated, due to its stout resistance to the Manchus in the 17th century. The slaughter was awesome. As a result, Han Chinese from all over the south rushed in, especially the Hakkas. Hakka means 'guest people'. They were originally from the Northern provinces and drifted south when invaders pushed them out in the early centuries, thus becoming 'guests'. Many of them, including my own family, thus came to Sichuan and here prospered and acquired that particular buoyancy, that spirit of hard work and survival, obvious to anyone spending any time here.

Sichuan women are far more active than in North China. The Hakka, being always on the move, did not bind the feet of their women. Hakka women are the most industrious and capable in China, and this tradition has persisted. Even when walking on the street a Sichuan woman continues knitting a wool jacket . . . so as not to waste time.

With this combination of abundance and vigour, Sichuan is modernising better than other provinces. To begin with, the war years left here some infrastructure of industry, particularly in Chongqing. Chongqing today produces tractors, watches, bicycles, motorcycles, electronic goods, steel, generators. It has coal and iron. The coal in Sichuan is just 3 metres below ground. Many peasants 'mine' coal simply by digging it up with a spade. There are enough engineers, geologists, and technical personnel locally to maintain a modernising process. It was in Sichuan that the first reforms in agriculture, begun in 1978, took place; today's Prime Minister, Mr. Zhao Zeyang, was then Governor of the Province. And the results were excellent — within a year, production of oil, eggs, ducks and meat had doubled or tripled.

It is also here that the system of individual enterprise began . . . and is growing well. The old-fashioned hotels sent their managers to Hong Kong to learn how to run hotels, something which was not done even in Beijing. Sichuan has also sizable potential in food canning industries. Alas, because of transport difficulties, the food canned here goes to Shanghai, where the labels, it is said, are changed to: 'Made in Shanghai', which irritates the Sichuan people a great deal. It is the same with Sichuan silk; silk probably originally came from here. Even today it is the best silk in China, weighed, not measured, since it goes by purity of stuff. Yet to have it shaped into clothes the silk has to go to Shanghai . . . although in Chengdu there is an enterprise which wants to design fashion clothes.

What more can one say: that this is also a tourist paradise, for the tourist who loves the hand of man upon the earth. For here are old, old temples, 2,000 years in existence. Taoist temples surrounded by rare trees like the gingko and the metasequoia, once believed extinct. Here are nature preserves, not only for the panda, but also for the wawayu , the water salamander, unknown elsewhere.

Here are customs unknown in other parts of China, and festivals full of mirth and colour. Here family planning began the earliest of all, way back in 1957. Sichuan holds the record in male vasectomies — two million out of a total of four million in the whole of China.

The province is peppered with Buddhist relics, such as the wonderful sculptures of Da Zu, near Chongqing. There are houses of famous poets, there are Han Dynasty tombs, there is a whole hill carved into one single Buddha 233 feet high at Leshan, 120 kilometres from Chengdu. It dates back to the eighth century and a special drainage system within the statue keeps it in excellent condition. Here on the fifth day of the fifth lunar month (May-June) are held Dragon Boat races, where women compete with men in a duck-snatching contest. Everyone swims to catch live ducks tossed in the water. In North Sichuan is scenery to rival Switzerland, and in the West gleaming, unscaled, 5,000 metre snow peaks. Here is a valley of the dinosaurs, full of their bones, where the largest dinosaur in existence was discovered and now stands in the museum of the Geology University in Chengdu.

In Chengdu are public dancing places in the parks; the girls here follow avidly the fashions of French magazines, imported I do not know how. Films that are not shown in Beijing are shown in Chongqing and other cities of the Four Streams . . .

What of the future? "Just give us transport, communications, electricity . . . we'll manage" say the Sichuanese. The province has established its own links with the West; delegations have gone to America and to Europe; a provincial airline will fly directly to Hong Kong. There will be an exhibition of Sichuan relics in the USA next year . . . Sichuan's factories comprise a sizeable amount of national defense plants, which are to be modernised. Anyone who has not seen Sichuan, the lively heart of China, has missed a great deal.

YUNNAN — South of the Clouds.

FROM Sichuan a railway built in the late 1960's goes south, plunging into hitherto almost inaccessible regions. In winter aeroplanes are haphazard. From November to February a thick quilt of fog covers the Land of Abundance, a blanket which ends suddenly as we approach the autonomous region of the Cool Mountains, the land of the Yi.

The railway is a great piece of engineering, for as we go along we cross several hundred bridges over streams and plunge in and out of several hundred tunnels. Here the mountains crisscross each other and as the tail of the train emerges from one tunnel the head is already plunging into the dark interior of another.

All this area is bewildering in the diversity of its ethnic groups. Each has its own history, a history which also forms part of China's history. Which is the reason why, on the train, there is not only a team of seismologists (because the area is earthquake prone) but also geologists, mineralogists, biologists, botanists, social scientists, linguists . . . All over the Southwest I shall find these eager scholars, collecting material, both from oral history (so many of the national minorities have no written language) and from artefacts, carvings, engravings, forgotten temples, unrecorded traditions.

After some 40 hours on the train I have reached the Cool Mountains, and here are the Yi, (1.2 million Yi in China), who have their own autonomous administrative unit.

45. Checkers players, Xian – Shaanxi

46.   Checkers player, Renmin Park – Shanghai

47. Transporting coal, Yangtse River – Sichuan

48. Bat wing junks on Yangtse River, Chongqing – Sichuan

49.   At play – Beijing

50.   River ferry on Yangtse River – Sichuan

51.   Chengdu – Sichuan

52.   Red Riding Hood in Tiananmen Square – Beijing

(Following page)
53.   Storm scene – South Sichuan

54.   Fengjie, Yangtse River – Sichuan

55.   Xian – Shaanxi

56. Qianling tombs, Xian – Shaanxi

· 57. Money changer at Ming Tombs – Beijing

The Yis have their own hieroglyphic written language.

Their agriculture is still of the 'slash and burn' type, except that they are forbidden to do so, as they damage nature's coverage. They have large flocks of goats, sheep and some cattle. For the last three decades the government has tried to educate them in some modern ways, building for them new houses, distributing blankets, opening schools. But the Yis continue to sleep outside the houses, and sell the blankets when they come to the city to trade (buying bright cloth, beads, thermos flasks and Chinese orange jam made in Sichuan, which grows excellent oranges). They stay on the higher slopes and though a lot of money is ploughed into trying to improve the herds, a Yi official, who actually volunteered to join the Long March when Mao Tsetung's armies passed through this district in early 1935, says to me: "My people do not change easily."

The Yis had a slave/aristocrat society, and their books tell them that they are 'Heavenborn'. We go into the mountains to visit a Yi settlement; the women wear pleated skirts, embroidered jackets. Here on the rocks are carved strange figures of no identifiable Buddhist creed; they may belong to pre-Buddhist or Shamanist cults. There is a museum where Yi art is exhibited — small lacquer pots, lacquer cups mounted upon the feet of eagles and hawks that the Yis catch and kill; shields and spears, also lacquered. "They love red and black lacquer" says the curator. I meet a Yi doctor, who stays with his people, hopes to train many young doctors. At first the Yi refused vaccination, refused to come to the clinics. "Of course the problem still is tuberculosis" the doctor says. The Yis have no resistance to the disease.

Down from the Yi autonomous region, to Yunnan, South of the Clouds. To meet the Bai and the Bonan, the Dai and the Dong, the Dongxing and the Jingpo, the She and the Li, the Hani and the Miao. Black, white, red, blue, flowery and cowry shell Miao.

The Miao spread over a very large area in earlier centuries; cowry shells have been found in neolithic settlements in North China. Marco Polo, who was here too, wrote: "They use cowry shells for money . . . they make collars for dogs out of them . . ."

In this province of 380,000 sq kilometres, population around 24 million, there are 19 national minorities. I must not confuse the Nasi (spelled Norsu by some) with the Yis, who are here too; nor the Ge with the Miao, and as for the Yao, the Li, the Lisu and the Wa — I only know them when they tell me, proudly, who they are.

Here in Yunnan are also the Hui. Everywhere in China one meets Muslims. Although they are said to be no more than 12 to 15 million, I think they are probably more. Certainly in Beijing itself, one whole district of nearly 200,000 people, before 1949, was Muslim. There are entire Hui villages on the road to the remarkable Stone Forest, a tourist attraction. Their cleanliness, and of course absence of pigs, makes them distinct.

Marco Polo again: "Here be many merchants and craftsmen of many races:

Saracens (Arabs), idolaters, and some Nestorian Christians . . ."

The earliest record of Yunnan, named South of the Clouds because the blanket of fog over its neighbour Sichuan does not reach it, is given by the historian Suma Tsian (141 to 87 b.c.), an account of the topography, the tribes and their customs, but intercourse dated back a few centuries earlier. It was once again the Mongols, who in 1254 a.d. integrated Yunnan, as they integrated Tibet in 1260 a.d., but there were uprisings against the rulers from Beijing, especially from the Muslims, until the 19th century.

Here too, like everywhere else, the Communist government has tried hard to conciliate the minorities; to uplift their standard of living, not only with subsidies, a health network and schools (in their own as well as the Han language), but also with privileges which the Han do not have. Throughout the Southwest, as in the North and Northwest, there are institutes for national minorities, to train cadres who can then run the local affairs of their own people. This policy seems to work. There is, in Yunnan, a good atmosphere between the races. What is especially striking is the freedom of many of the women from the minorities. I am told that this is because their societies were somewhat matriarchal until recently. Certainly I saw here, on several occasions, something never seen in Han China. I saw women pushing carts in which their husbands sat . . . and even, once, a woman with her husband on her back, scaling a hill . . . "It's because men are so frail" I was told.

The capital city, Kunming, is 1,800 metres up and since Yunnan is sub-tropical this means balmy weather most of the year round. It was founded following a meeting (round 300 b.c.) between the Han and the local people, who were very friendly. Below Kunming is a lovely lake, with superb landscape, alas spoiled during the cultural revolution when the banks were turned into fields to plant more rice, thus destroying not only the scenery, but also the fish, through seepage of chemical fertilisers. Friend Marco Polo had already recorded, seven centuries ago, that here the fish were "the best in the world".

Not to be missed in Kunming is the museum, where there is the most extraordinary collection of Yunnan bronzes, a collection now world famous. The patterns are utterly different from anything else seen in China and the art is superb. Here can be seen the original drums of bronze, found in Borneo, and called 'Dayak' drums, because the Dayak tribes of Borneo use them. But they came from Yunnan, as did many of the ethnic groups of southeast Asia, including the Malays of Malaya, who freely acknowledge that they "came down from Yunnan" round the tenth century.

Yunnan also has a large Thai (Dai) population, whose style of living and language is entirely like that of Thailand today. Their festivals, including the Feast of Lights, and the throwing of coloured water upon each other to celebrate the New Year, are Burmese-Thai, and not Han Chinese.

During the Second World War, Yunnan was the back door through which supplies came to Free China, the government refugeed in Sichuan province, by road and by air. A large American Air Force contingent lived in Kunming. The famous Burma Road was built on an old road which had existed for many centuries, and which was actually also a Silk Road, bringing silk from Sichuan to Burma, Bengal and India. The road traverses what was once known as the Kingdom of Zhao, with its capital near a city known today as Dali. Here live the Bai, a stalwart race, handsome and capable. Their autonomous area produces a great deal of milk from excellent cattle, milk dried and exported. I went to see them, and visited the marble workshops of Dali; marble flecked and streaked, much prized by the overseas Chinese who love to have pieces, representing landscapes, clouds or strange beasts, encrusted in their tables and chairs. Near a beautiful lake, called the Ear Lake (it is thus shaped) which receives 18 streams, there was a small area with old trees and ponds, where butterflies gather to mate . . . butterflies of splendid colours and all sizes, a wonderful sight. Alas, because of new factories, industries and pollution, the butterflies have gone elsewhere.

All along the road from Dali are marvellous old temples; very sacred, very revered. Some of them were wrecked during the Cultural Revolution, but have been repaired. Burmese used to cross the border every year to worship here.

GUIZHOU — Where Dogs Bark at the Sun.
GUANGXI — Where Chinese Painting Comes Alive.

THE provinces of Guangxi, a name which means Ample West, and Guizhou, Precious Land, both have 'autonomous' zones to a very large degree. In Guangxi live the Zhuang, who are over ten million and very much like the Han, in clothes, language and customs, although they still benefit from some privileges. According to a recent report, the Zhuang are merging so quickly with the Hans that the privilege of having more than one child no longer applies to them.

Guangxi (230,000 sq kilometres, population about 30 million, 40 per cent of whom are minorities) is well known to tourists, especially the area round the city of Guilin, Cassia Forest (it used to be odorous with cassia blossom in spring). A fabulous landscape, blue and green promontories, spires and pyramids and peaks, which are actually mountain-size boulders rising straight from the ground; not mountains, but the giant stones of an ocean bed lifted upwards. Below ground are enormous caves, with underground waterfalls and streams and the whole area is tunnelled with sink holes and caverns. This karst formation is found throughout the province and continues into the sea, the Bay of Along.

Upon the Li river, which belts Cassia Forest, thin boats skim, carrying cormorants which swoop into the water to catch fish. They wear a ring round the neck to prevent them swallowing their catch. Along the banks are small villages with waving, fan-like bamboo groves, and small boys perched upon giant water buffaloes. Idyllic, beautiful . . . and exactly like a Chinese painting. Here one knows that the painters did not dream up the mountains and waterfalls and trees they painted. They reproduced exactly the almost dreamlike surrealist beauty of Cassia Forest.

Here too will come change . . . and factories. There is a dam, with hydro-electric power. One hopes that there will not be pollution, destroying all the beauty, the purity, of this lovely land.

Guizhou is a province almost unknown, seldom visited, though probably one of China's wealthiest with regard to mineral resources — phosphorus, silver, manganese, copper. It is also one of the wettest. I never remember a day there without some rain, and the bed sheets in the hotels were always damp . . . "The sun appears so rarely that the dogs bark when they see it", is said of Guiyang, the capital. Guizhou province (174,000 sq kilometres, population round 20 million), holds about one and a half million Miaos, and 25 per cent of the inhabitants are minorities.

It is in Guizhou that one begins to love the Miao; for their skills, for their physical handsomeness, for their spirit and sense of beauty. The Miao are evolving rapidly — one finds Miao people in all the big cities. Some of China's famous painters of today are Miao and so are musicians at the academies in Sichuan and in Shanghai.

For a while suppressed, on the ground of 'immorality', I hear that the courtship customs of the Miao have been revived. In autumn the unwed girls climb stout poles, whose ladder steps are actually planted swords. From the pole tops they throw a ball of coloured cloth to the young man they have chosen . . . there used to be trial periods of free sex before marriage. I do not know whether this still occurs. However, courtship is a very important matter. The young man and his chosen (or choosing) female partner will sing to each other, sing love poems which they compose. Wit, a lovely voice, impassioned lyrics, certainly have a lot to do with the choosing, which is done in front of a critical audience. To see a Miao woman bedecked with her heavy silver jewellery, her embroidered skirts, jackets, bag (everything is embroidered), is a lovely sight.

In Guizhou is a little town called Tsunyi, famous because here in January 1935 Mao Tsetung was selected to lead the harassed, dispirited remnants of the Red Army fleeing before the massive hunt of Chiang Kaishek. Here the soldiers stopped and asked for Mao. Now he would lead them, onwards through this province, and the region of the Yis, and the western part of Sichuan, always choosing the sparsely populated minorities areas, until he reached the loess region, and there, in caves dug out of the loess, began to forge the strength, and the battalions, which led to victory 14 years later.

58. Fuli village entrance – Guanxi

59.   Tiananmen Square – Beijing

60. Courtyard to outer walls of the imperial city – Beijing

61. Wuzhou – Guangdong

62. Winter rooftops – Shanghai

(Following pages)

63. Han card player, Renmin Park – Shanghai

64. Cormorant fisherman at dusk, Li River – Guangxi

68.　Tai-Chi by West Lake, Hangzhou – Zhejiang

Mao and the Han soldiers with him received kindness and help from many minorities, and once Mao came to power, the policy of giving national minorities many privileges, of helping them both financially and educationally, was implemented. In Old China, the national minorities had been badly treated, with contempt if not worse, by the Han majority. Now all this has changed.

Today, attending universities out of each 10,000 of their populations are 24.1 from the minorities and 8.8 from The Han majority. The family planning programme allows them more children than the Han. In the past seven years seven billion yuan went to one autonomous region, Tibet, and other billions to the Yi, the Mongols . . .

From the diverse, capricious, mosaic China of mountains and deserts and high plateaus to China of the plains.

Here is man-made, man-shaped land, canals, lakes, miniature enchanting gardens which in their exquisite proportion scoop perspective as if they dealt with miles instead of yards — and nowhere here can one ever be alone. Not only crowded cities, but a crowded countryside, with villages at every turn; with roads along which grain is spread to dry — tarmac upon which grain is spread so that the wheels of vehicles will help to thresh it.

Right next to Guangxi, the Ample West, is GUANGDONG, Ample East, a province utterly different from its neighbour. Guangdong (area 220,000 sq kilometres, population over 55 million) was earliest influenced by the West. Its capital, then known as Canton, was, since the end of the 17th century, where British, French and other 'devils from the oceans' were allowed to have 'factories', which meant godowns, and houses — an enclave which still today exists. Shameen Island still shows 19th century houses of the British merchants.

The province is totally a Han province, speaking the Cantonese dialect which is actually the Han language which was spoken by Confucius 2,500 years ago. Guangdong is the province with the highest income and productivity after the Shanghai area, and the fastest modernisation — for a simple reason. The Cantonese have the greatest number of 'overseas' Chinese of all of China's provinces. Fully 60% of the 25 million Chinese overseas come from this single region. As a result, money has kept flowing in, since family bonds are extremely strong. It is in Guangdong that one of the four experimental 'free zones', where foreign investments and companies are allowed a free hand, is sited next to Hong Kong; and Hong Kong is geographically and linguistically part of the province.

Another province with an enormous number of overseas Chinese is FUKIEN, also, like Guangdong, with a seacoast and many ports. And further up the seacoast income per head is the highest in China — in JIANGSU, with the immense 12 million strong port of Shanghai.

All these coastal provinces are outperforming the rest of China, producing a disequilibrium in investment potential and therefore in income per capita. However, it is certain that foreign companies will choose to come here, with access to the sea, rather than in the transport-lacking inland regions.

Investment here will produce quick returns — will the returns (or profit, to use a word which no Chinese is ashamed of using, socialism or not) then be used to help the more backward regions, especially with reference to an infra structure of transport and energy?

I walk by the beautiful West Lake of Hangzhou, one of China's great tourist resorts. Everything here is man-made, man-shaped, including the lake, with its millions of carp — healthy looking and voracious — and fearless red carp, from which the goldfish in all their varieties were produced by the Chinese before they had heard of genetic manipulation.

I visit the factories of Shanghai, where the ideogram is now adapted to the computer; where, in joint venture with a Hong Kong company, China is producing a computer which can alternate six languages, including Chinese and Greek, and store memories in all six languages at once.

China of the plains, surging forward. Will it help the other China, the China of the mountains, the deserts, the plateaus, to catch up . . . and how long will it take? Will this prosperous seaboard China invest in curbing the deserts, which threaten the whole of the North and may turn 35 per cent of the land into arid sand?

IN Beijing, at each meeting of the National Assembly, the minorities are there; their numbers exceed the quota allowed Han representatives, otherwise some of them would never be there at all. How would, for instance, the Wa, less than five thousand, otherwise have two representatives? In this and many other ways, the Chinese government is trying to foster harmony and good relations, between the Han and the others, who altogether number round 80-85 million, 8 per cent of the billion and more of China's inhabitants.

"China is a symphony orchestra" said one Han scholar to me. "Some have a big instrument to play, and some only a small one . . . but all are necessary, all must play together, to achieve a successful melody."

After travelling in this other China, one sees Beijing with a new eye: one sees it as not only Han Chinese, but also Mongol, Manchu and even Turkoman . . . the capital of a multi-nationed State, trying to motivate every one of its so diverse citizens to progress. And one wants to return, again and again, to see these other Chinese, the Wa, the Uighurs, the Yis, the Miao, who have also made China what she is.

70. Near Xian – Shaanxi

71. Foshan – Guangdong

72.   Near Yangshuo – Guangxi

73. Rice crop, Yangshuo – Guangxi

74. At Qiongzhu Temple, Kunming – Yunnan

75. Carp in West Lake, Hangzhou – Zhejiang

76.　Yi needleworker, Shiling – Yunnan

77.　Miao tribeswomen, Kunming – Yunnan

(Following page)
78.   Sunset on West River – Guangdong

THE PHOTOGRAPHS

1. A field of rapeseed just south of Lhasa. Irrigation since 1950 has allowed cropping of rape and wheat in the southern Tibetan valleys.

2. Potala palace viewed from the roof of the Jokhang temple. This palace was the former residence of the Dalai Lama, spiritual head of Tibet. It was begun in the 8th century but not completed until the 13th century. Contains 1,100 rooms.

3. A camel train travels the ancient 'silk route' across the Gansu desert near Dunhuang.

4. This rice field flourishes right in the midst of suburban Chengdu, Sichuan province.

5. Most Lhasa dwellers have jobs in offices, schools, shops, etc. but on the streets the burning of offerings combined with government induced burning of brush to spare timber together with the traditional Tibetan fuel of yak dung, creates a continual smoke haze.

6. Fuelling a juniper hearth of a stupa-like erection in front of Tibet's holiest site — the Jokhang temple.

7. Gyangze, once the third largest town in Tibet, sits astride the main trade route to Nepal. Every monastery in Tibet is a stone fortress with streets, walls and houses. This is the famous Citadel, site of a British attack in 1904. The lamas were traders and many monasteries were situated to suit. It is alleged the lamas waxed wealthy at the expense of the populace.

8. Prayer flags above the Polkor monastery in Gyangze. The stupa in the centre of the monastery is the largest in Tibet.

10. Pilgrims in a teahouse specially erected by Han Chinese to cater for them.

11. Meat being roasted in an alleyway beside Jokhang Temple, using a burner westerners use for removing paint or similar.

13. Uighur girl probably of Tadjik ancestry, near the Abakh Hoja. Note colourful, smart dress and scarf.

14. Few young Tibetans are being recruited as monks. This one is selling prayer tracts which are hung as festoons or on rocks at the roadside, there being a marked lack of trees in Tibet.

15. Young goat herders near Lake Yamdrok Yamtso. The southern area of Tibet is capable of much development as pasture land. Unfortunately, there are only about 2 Tibetans per square kilometre, the infant mortality being very high.

16. Urumqi, capital of Xinjiang, has both Han (in background) old buildings and Islamic architecture. The trees in Urumqi were planted in the 18th century by the general who incorporated the New Domain into China. This building graces the Renmin (People's) Park in the central city.

17. Summer camp for some Kazakh herdspeople at Tianchi (the Lake of Heaven). Note their portable skin yurts or huts.

18. Han boy, but wearing a Uighur hat.

19. Shaving the head of a customer probably lice ridden after a long journey. This fierce exponent does a flourishing trade.

20. Hami melons are famous all over the East.

21. If the baize surface of a pool table cannot be replaced there is always a piece of the locally manufactured carpet.

22. The spread of television and nationwide sports competitions has infected the Uighur population reflected in the imagination and inventiveness of youngsters at 'ping pong' under very difficult circumstances in Renmin Square.

23. Kazakh herdsman and son at the Lake of Heaven in the Tian Shan mountain range.

24. The great Sugongta Mosque of Turfan restored in 1979. To it flock Uighurs from all over the province. The architecture is typical of the area — a mixture of styles which greatly interested the Aga Khan on his visit to the area during which visit Han Suyin was the chief speaker. Here the old keeper finds a peaceful moment for prayer after all the tourists have departed.

25. Restoration of a Han nationality mosque. In Xinjiang there are mosques for the Hui who speak Chinese and mosques for the Uighurs, Tadjiks, Kazakhs, etc. who speak languages akin to the Turkish.

26. There are markets in Urumqi selling Chinese goods, notably silk, which is now also woven and dyed in patterns which the minorities prefer (stripes and flowers) and in colours more vivid than the Han, who prefer pastel, subdued colours.

27. Drying bricks — temperatures often reach 47°C in Turfan.

28. Early morning activity as traders gather for the Sunday market overseen by the huge statue of Mao. Farmers still use donkey carts. The Uighur people were once called 'the high wheeled people' because their carts had exceptionally big wheels.

29. It is from Kashgar onwards in Xinjiang and in Tibet that China is promoting the development of new breeds of sheep, including cashmere of which she has become a major producer.

30. Descendants of Arab settlers (note the features), trading in the free market near Urumqi bus station. The markets attract traders from all over China and neighbouring states such as Pakistan, selling everything from camels to clothes.

31/32. On part of the old silk route in the Gansu desert, near Dunhuang, an area still plied by lines of Bactrian (two humped camels) and the ubiquitous donkey.

33. The children of Kashgar are full of fun and enterprise and have an uncanny knack of detecting tourists and devoting attention to them.

34. Turfan is renowned since the 5th century for its dancers and its music. Here Uighurs are performing under vine trellises. Kashgar, it can be noted, has exported its stringed musical instruments for many centuries.

35. Xinjiang is famous for its grapes but first the vines must be pruned.

36. The carved cliffs and Bilingisi Buddhist caves on the Yellow River which the Silk Road out of Gansu followed.

37. Interior of a Bilingisi cave dating back to the 5th century and the western Qin dynasty.

38. Sichuan province produces over 1,000 different species of medicinal herbs, fungi etc. and sells its herbal and animal (including Pangolin) remedies all over S.E. Asia.

39. Upper reaches of the Yellow River. The cliffs are soft sandstone and erosion has transformed them into strange shapes.

40. Early morning light filters through a smoke filled sleeper carriage.

41. This line to Golmud is planned to extend through to Lhasa as a part of China's move to her west, as it gradually reveals its enormous wealth.

42/44. The Terracotta Warrior ballet illustrates the enormous capability of the Chinese with dance and stage. The thousands of ceramic figures found in the tomb of the First Emperor, Qin Shihuangdi (221 to 207 b.c.), attract world wide attention. Xian, sited in the loess region of North China, was one of several northern capitals of the Chinese dynasties; notably later under the Tang. All around the loess area between Gansu and Beijing excavations are proceeding, revealing palaeolithic and neolithic sites (more than 5,000 so far). The ceramic soldiers of the tomb of the First Emperor are a major discovery. The First Emperor is also credited with having 'built' the Great Wall. Actually, he consolidated it, using a million people in extending it eastwards, recruiting labour even as far down as the province of Guangxi and Guangdong.

43. The Peking Opera is a marvellous kaleidoscope of dance, singing, acrobatics and fire eating. Many of the scenes are based on heroic epics of battles with the invading barbarians from the north.

45. Sidewalk activities such as this are a very common recreation throughout China. These players are in the fascinating area around the Drum Tower in Xian.

47. Coal is available only a few feet down on the banks of the Yangtse. Using the human chain method these small peasant mines are now greatly encouraged because they discourage chopping down trees for fuel. Barges transport the coal to sales points.

48. Bat wing junks hug the banks of the Yangtse and are used mainly in the more open regions of the river.

49. Children the world over like to play soldiers!

50. A young worker returning to his work unit in Anhui province by river ferry on the Yangtse.

52. A toddler in Tiananmen Square during winter.

54. All towns on the Yangtse have these stone staircases descending 25 metres and more to the river allowing for the devastating flood rises that may occur.

55. Brush painting is indeed an art. The ideogram, which is an enduring value in China and is now adapted to the computer, lends itself to a thousand artistic pursuits. There are contests for calligraphy held throughout China almost every month. There are a lot of modernists amongst her many street artists. This man attracts much attention close to the old mosque at the Drum Tower.

56. A guardian stone statue at one of the many excavations in the loess regions.

57. At the entrance to the Ming Tombs outside Beijing a money changer plies his trade.

58. Ancient entrance gate to Fuli on the banks of the Li River.

59. Kite flying in the right wind conditions is a national activity throughout the country.

60. These outer walls boxed in the Forbidden City.

62. Old city roofs. The population in main cities has become so dense that many areas are being torn down and replaced with multistorey modern buildings. This area of single storey houses probably houses more than 5 people per room.

64. Cormorant fishing is only practised in Guangxi and in Guangdong.

65. The Great Wall here has been repaired and most of it dates back only to the 15th century. Further west some portions go back to the third century B.C.

66. Some of the tormented landscape of the Karst region of Guangxi.

68. Tai chi or 'shadow boxing' is indulged in by all ages, any time, anywhere.

69. This beautiful frangipani graces a quiet corner of the Huaisheng Mosque, built 627 a.d.

72. View from Moon hill.

73. The Miao people of the northern valleys of Guangxi produce two crops of rice per year.

74. The Buddhist religion is widespread throughout China. The use of candles is to celebrate the anniversary of a dead ancestor.

75. Carp are found in large numbers in the milder climates of east and south China.

76/77. Amongst the Miao nationality the women do most of the work, including trading at free markets.

HAN SUYIN

HAN SUYIN is one of the best known writers in the world today. Her books are translated into 17 languages, including Chinese and Japanese. She has a diverse public, both for her fiction and romantic novels, and also for her research studies and books on China which comprise economics, politics and medical work. Anyone who wishes to understand China has to read Han Suyin. As the late Bertrand Russel remarked: "During the many hours I spent reading Han Suyin's books, I learnt more about China in an hour than I did in a whole year spent in that country."

HAN SUYIN is the daughter of a Chinese father and a Belgian mother. She grew up in Peking, and was moved by the poverty and sickness round her to take up medicine, despite her mother's disapproval. She entered Yenching University, and then obtained a scholarship to Belgium, where she completed her premedical studies (1936-38). In 1938 she returned to China, for as she says: "I could not stay in peace in Europe while China was being invaded by Japan." She married an ex-Sandhurst Chinese officer, and practised midwifery in the interior during the war. From her experiences (1938-1942) she wrote her first book, DESTINATION CHUNGKING. In 1942 her husband, Tang Paohuang, was promoted military attache to London and Han Suyin accompanied him to England. In 1945 her husband returned to China, where he was killed in the civil war in 1947. Han Suyin remained in England till the end of 1948 to complete her medical studies, working in her spare time to support herself and her adopted daughter, Yungmei. She spent a year as a house surgeon in London (1948) then in 1949 accepted a medical post in Hongkong. There she wrote the love story A MANY—SPLENDOURED THING. In 1952 she went to Malaya and practised medicine there till 1964. Her novel AND THE RAIN MY DRINK is still acclaimed as the best novel on Malaya. In 1956, Han Suyin went to Nepal to attend the coronation of the King of Nepal and wrote THE MOUNTAIN IS YOUNG. Afterwards followed more novels; THE FOUR FACES, on Cambodia, CAST THE SAME SHADOW and WINTER LOVE. From 1956 onwards she returned to China where the late

Premier, Zhou Enlai, received her frequently. She began a five-volume combined autobiography and history of China, which traces what happened to her family and to herself through the many twists and turns of the Chinese revolution. Between 1964 and 1968 three books of this series were published and won universal acclaim. They are THE CRIPPLED TREE, A MORTAL FLOWER, BIRDLESS SUMMER. Han Suyin completed the fourth and fifth volumes which cover the years 1949 to 1976 MY HOUSE HAS TWO DOORS and PHOENIX HARVEST by 1979. She has since published a novel which is a national best-seller TILL MORNING COMES in 1982, and another novel, THE ENCHANTRESS, published in the United States in January 1985.

From 1968 to 1975 Han suyin was engaged in a monumental work, the life of Chairman Mao Tsetung and its impact on China, in two volumes, entitled THE MORNING DELUGE and WIND IN THE TOWER. These were completed and an additional chapter, covering Mao's death and the downfall of his wife and her acolytes, was published in paperback series in 1977 and 1978.

Since the early 1960's she has been on regular lecture tours to the United States, winning acclaim at international seminars on the Far East, and to all European countries and Japan as well as to India, Egypt and Africa.

In Malaya, Han Suyin also taught contemporary Asian literature for three years (1958-1961) at Nanyang University in Singapore.

At McGill University, Montreal, she was the recipient of the Beatty scholarship. This scholarship is given to persons whose contribution has been of outstanding merit and value to promote understanding between people.

In France, the Paris Municipality has struck a special medal to commemorate Han Suyin and her work. Such an honour is rarely given to an author. Albert Einstein and Andre Malraux are other recipients of similar medals.

Besides these activities, Han Suyin is also a regular lecturer at the French Military Academy, lecturing on Chinese military affairs.

THE PHOTOGRAPHERS

Mike Langford works out of Rapport Photo Agency and the bustle of the Sydney commercial scene and his services are ever in demand. An indefatigable worker, he travels extensively within Australia and internationally. He has won many professional photographers' gold awards and his work has appeared in five different books during the last year. He is acknowledged as a real 'up and coming' force in Australian photography.

Geoff Mason has built himself a log cabin under the Southern Alps of New Zealand from which he runs photographic safaris and schools. He has worked on a number of books and publications including a major contribution to the very successful 'A Day in the Life of New Zealand'. He taught photography for three years at Wellington Polytechnic worked as a 'stills' on films, has won many awards and scholarships, including one for study in the U.S.A. and another for photography in Europe, Bahrain and Sri Lanka. As well he has photographed extensively throughout the Pacific.

We are grateful for the assistance afforded by Access Travel, Sydney